LOOKING FORWARD
GLANCING BACK

LOOKING FORWARD
GLANCING BACK

NORTHWEST
DESIGNER
CRAFTSMEN
AT 50

LLOYD E. HERMAN

WHATCOM MUSEUM OF
HISTORY & ART

©2004, Northwest Designer Craftsmen

Published in association with the Whatcom Museum of History & Art, Bellingham, Washington

Distributed by the University of Washington Press
Seattle and London

ISBN 0-295-98431-7

Published in conjunction with the exhibition
Looking Forward, Glancing Back: Northwest Designer Craftsmen at 50
June 13, 2004 –Oct. 23, 2004
Whatcom Museum of History & Art, Bellingham, Washington

essay ©Lloyd Herman

Designed by Phil Kovacevich

Photo credits: All photos courtesy of the artist, except as noted.
Page 12, Eric Franklin; Page 10, 13, 14 (bottom), 15 (top), 16 (bottom), 17, 18 (top) Roger Schreiber; Page 14 (top) Emily Welsch; Page 32 (top) Ken Wagner; Page 33 (top) Bill Bachhuber; Page 34 (bottom) Tom Holt; Page 39 (bottom) Carl Bortolami; Page 42 (top) Brooke Greiner; Page 45 (top) Jerry McCollum; Page 46 (bottom) Lynn Thompson; Page 47 (top) Frank Ross, (bottom) Bill Bachhuber; Page 48 (bottom) Bill Smythe; Page 51 (top) Kevin McGowan; Page 55 (bottom) Jack McLin; Page 57 (bottom) Richard Nicol; Page 58 (bottom) Denise Snyder; Page 60 (top) Roger Schreiber, (bottom) Kevin McGowan; Page 61 (top) Robert Gibeau; Page 62 (bottom) LightWorks Photography; Page 65 (top) Chris Arend; Page 67 (bottom) Jerry McCollum; Page 69 (bottom) Bill Bachhuber; Page 70 (top) Mason McCuddin; Page 71 (bottom) Emily Welch; Page 77 (top) Duncan Price

Printed in China

CONTENTS

FOREWORD   7
Thomas A. Livesay, Lisa Van Doren
Whatcom Museum of History & Art

INTRODUCTION   9
Larry Metcalf
President, Northwest Designer Craftsmen

LOOKING FORWARD, GLANCING BACK   11
Northwest Designer Craftsmen at 50
Lloyd Herman

PLATES   23

CHECKLIST OF THE EXHIBITION   77

FOREWORD

COLLABORATING WITH NORTHWEST DESIGNER CRAFTSMEN fits perfectly with the goals of the Whatcom Museum of History & Art—providing advocacy for regional and local artists while advancing awareness and appreciation of the arts in our community. Partnering with a like-minded institution such as NWDC has been a rewarding experience, and we are proud to present this carefully chosen selection of contemporary and historic works of craft.

Organizing a major exhibition and catalogue is never an easy task, and only through the dedication and assistance of many people can it be successful. We are grateful for the generous support of Peoples Bank and the City of Bellingham, whose sponsorship made this exhibition possible.

We have been fortunate to work with a consummate expert and scholar in craft, Lloyd Herman. As guest curator, Lloyd has selected some of the finest examples available of historic and contemporary craft to tell the story of NWDC. We are grateful for his professionalism and wealth of knowledge and for his insightful essay in this catalogue.

Also key to the success of this ambitious exhibition were the efforts of several staff members at the Whatcom Museum. Special thanks go to Director of Exhibitions Scott Wallin, whose cohesive exhibition design gracefully brought together a wide array of diverse objects; Development Director Kathleen Iwersen, without whose fund-raising efforts this exhibition would not be possible; and Mary Jo Maute, whose early involvement in organizing the exhibition helped get the project off to an energetic and ambitious start.

Our sincere appreciation goes to Phil Kovacevich for his elegant design of this catalogue. Laura Iwasaki's skillful edits helped clarify the publication. As a permanent record of the exhibition, the catalogue ensures that the ideas and artworks presented in the show will continue to promote the cultural dialogue regarding the role of contemporary crafts in the Northwest long after the exhibition closes.

Finally, we thank the NWDC members themselves. The joy and passion these artists bring to their creations is evident in the superb craftsmanship that only meticulous attention to detail, remarkable skill, and great patience can bring about. Their work is the result of years of dedicated practice, spent perfecting complicated techniques. The members' commitment to their crafts, their cooperation, and their professionalism are much appreciated. We are particularly grateful to Judy Barnes-Baker, Marie Hassett, and Larry Metcalf, who helped organize the exhibition and catalogue.

The Whatcom Museum is pleased to present this important exploration of craft in the Northwest and joins NWDC in celebrating the past as it continues to move forward. The future for crafts looks very bright.

THOMAS A. LIVESAY
Director
Whatcom Museum of History & Art

LISA VAN DOREN
Curator of Art
Whatcom Museum of History & Art

INTRODUCTION

FIFTY YEARS AGO, ten individuals came together, believing there was an important need for an organization dedicated to breaking down the barrier between "fine arts" and "craft." They established the original group Northwest Designer Craftsmen.

From the time of its founding, the mission of NWDC has been to promote quality of idea, design, and craftsmanship in all media. Artist-craftsmen from Alaska, Idaho, Montana, Oregon, and Washington apply for membership and are voted upon by their peers. Through their work, they must show an original approach to artistic philosophy and media. They must have established themselves as artists with résumés of accomplishments.

NWDC offers education on various facets of art by sponsoring public lectures and exhibitions that travel to galleries, schools, and museums throughout the Northwest. As teachers or committed artists and craftsmen, NWDC members conduct workshops and visit many regions of the country to further the interests of their organization.

In the 1990s, NWDC created "Living Treasures" video project, which documents and honors those members who have made a significant contribution to the arts and to the overall mission of NWDC. These Northwest individuals are captured in action as they render their valuable services to the art world.

Over the years, NWDC has published three catalogues of members' work. This catalogue is the fourth. It celebrates fifty years of accomplishments and anchors NWDC in the present. There have been many advances and changes in NWDC since its inception. All too often we forget how the organization of today has evolved from that original group of ten designer craftsmen. Transition may be difficult to imagine without looking forward, and glancing back helps put the present in context.

Fifty years seem like a long time in a person's life, even though the years go by quickly. But fifty years represent a short time in the flow of history. With the vision of the past and the excitement of the present, NWDC anticipates the next fifty years.

LARRY METCALF
President, NWDC

LOOKING FORWARD
GLANCING BACK

NORTHWEST DESIGNER
CRAFTSMEN AT 50

LLOYD E. HERMAN

FIFTY YEARS AGO, when Northwest Designer Craftsmen (NWDC) was founded, America was a simpler place. Television was in its infancy, and there was no digital anything, no cell phones, microwaves, or computers. We were on a wave of post–World War II optimism, fueled by new possibilities. For returning war veterans, there were opportunities to study the arts, subsidized by the GI Bill. Many chose to pursue ceramics or metalwork, and they enriched traditions in the craft field with new ideas. It was a period of prosperity, hope, and, with the end of the Korean War, economic vitality for the United States.

In the Northwest, the pioneer-era enterprise of making clothing, tools, simple furniture, and other necessities had long since died out, owing to the availability of a huge variety of manufactured goods. Such things as pots, tablecloths, and fabric did not have to be made by hand; the potter and the weaver did so by choice and then had to find those who would buy. By the 1950s, shortages of precious metals for the war effort had ended, and silversmiths were once again learning how to form teapots, punchbowls and traditional functional objects by forging and raising. However, the old styles were no longer enough to satisfy the taste for the new. In that atmosphere, nine Seattle craftmakers came together in 1954 and resolved to start a new membership organization. They were Russell Day, Henry Lin, Irene McGowan, Coralynn Pence, Ruth Penington, Lisel Salzer, Hella Skowronski, Evert Sodergren, and Robert Sperry. Their goals: to establish high standards of design and workmanship in the Northwest; to promote public interest in crafts and craftsmen; to provide a voice for all craftsmen in the Northwest area; and to provide a code of sound business methods among designer craftsmen.

The name, Northwest Designer Craftsmen, says a lot. Handmade things—crafts—had a heritage of usefulness, and that had not changed. The modern products being made by hand in the 1950s reflected a New England or a Southern traditional heritage. Here, in the states of

RUTH PENINGTON
Two Candlesticks
1963
Silver, uncut topaz
6½ x 4 in.

BETTY FEVES
Three Figures #4,
1955
Stoneware, handbuilt
18 x 12 in.

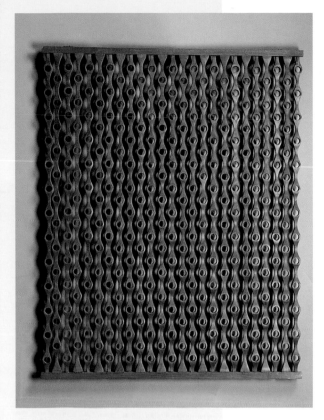

Washington, Oregon, Idaho, Montana, and Alaska, those perceived by the organization as "Northwest," craftspeople were not bound by traditions. Though there may have been a noticeable influence from Asia and Scandinavia in Seattle, craftmakers throughout the region felt free to design new products, unhindered by the designs of the past.

Gervais Reed, assistant director of the Henry Gallery at the University of Washington (now the Henry Art Gallery), writing in the catalog of the tenth Annual Northwest Craftsmen's Exhibition held there in 1962, pointed out that "crafts as we know them were introduced to the region through educational organizations—schools, colleges, federal art projects, weavers' guilds, and arts and crafts clubs. Most of these beginnings took place as recently as the 1930s when some of our teachers studied in Eastern schools such as Cranbrook where the new European tradition of the Bauhaus had put down roots in American soil....Others, influenced by modern art, discovered the ancient and the exotic: Peruvian textiles, Indian baskets, Mexican pottery, the folk arts of the Orient and Europe. All were imbued with the missionary ideas of 'Good Design,' of functional form and truth to materials which were advanced by books, traveling exhibitions, and art schools."

For the most part, the founders and members of NWDC were modernists who were aware of the new trends in architecture and the design of home furnishings. It is clear, from examining the objects made in the organization's first decade, that these works bore scant resemblance to "country" crafts, for which there was still a following elsewhere in the nation. These were not their grandmothers' crafts.

NWDC's founders included makers who were also influential teachers, whose advocacy of fresh design propelled their students toward this new modernism. Perhaps none of the founders exemplifies the idea of the designer craftsman better than Russell Day, then an instructor of

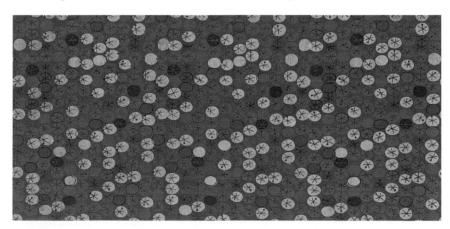

design and chair of the Division of Arts at Everett Junior College. Adept at several media, he created unique jewelry, metalwork, and stained glass as well as replicable designs for rugs and printed fabrics. He pioneered the integration of glass into concrete screening walls, which brought him regional commissions and led Dale Chihuly to seek his advice as mentor. His original jewelry remains significant, as does that of his former student, Donald Tompkins. Ruth Penington, professor of art at the University of Washington, was talented at creating new functional forms for the table in silver, and her dynamic jewelry—sometimes incorporating found objects—paved the way for her student, Ramona Solberg, to succeed her there. An early NWDC member from Montana, Frances Senska, taught ceramics at Montana State College (now Montana State University) to Rudy Autio and Peter Voulkos, two of the most influential artists of the twentieth century working in clay.

In the 1940s, these modern crafts were beginning to achieve notice, and respect. A national invitational craft exhibition at the Baltimore Museum of Art in that decade was followed by the first national, competitive, juried exhibition of American crafts in the early 1950s, sponsored by art museums in Philadelphia, San Francisco, and Chicago. This was the first acknowledgment, NWDC founding member Ruth Penington believed, that "craftsmen had been creative artists worthy of being shown in art museums."

In New York, patron Aileen Osborne Webb established the American Craftsmen's Cooperative Council (now American Craft Council) to further the field economically and educationally. Her effort led to the founding of a craft museum in New York (and a short-lived one in San Francisco), a periodical that could address the field, and a New York retail outlet for quality crafts, America House. The American Craft Council sponsored the first

(above left) RAMONA SOLBERG
Necklace
1953
Champleve enamel on silver
6 x 4½ x ⅛ in.

DONALD TOMPKINS
Bracelet Watch
ca. 1957
Silver, forged and fabricated; watch movement
3 x 2¼ x 2¼ in.

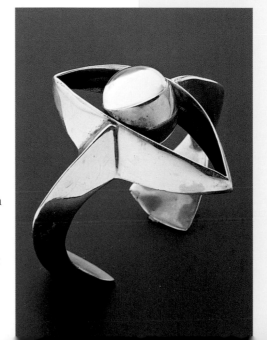

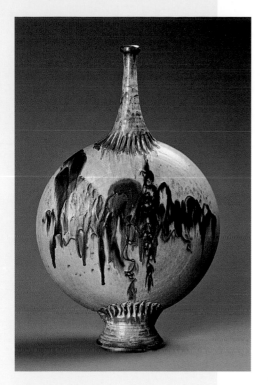

(above) ROBERT SPERRY
Untitled
1959
Stoneware thrown and altered,
glazed
24 x 15 x 6 in.

(right) KEN SHORES
Little Red I
1962
Stoneware, handbuilt, acrylic paint
20 in. high

*"About 1957 a restless change
became evident in pottery. Oddly
shaped, strangely decorated and
roughly constructed pottery appeared
among the entries, like creatures
from another world. These were the
work of serious and skillful potters
who had evidently turned their
backs on 'good design' in the traditional sense to search for something
else from clay and fire. This direction has become stronger each year,
until today it is the functional, con-
servative pot which is exceptional. It
also served to blur and then obliter-
ate the distinction between 'pottery'
and 'ceramic sculpture.'"*

—GERVAIS REED, 1962

national conferences of craftsmen, which encouraged interregional friendships and enabled participants to share and spread information. (Such networking became global when Webb also helped to establish the World Crafts Council.) NWDC provided a similar forum for discussion and sharing in the Northwest.

From its inception, NWDC accepted as members only craftspeople whose work was perceived to be of "professional" quality, whether or not they were able to make a living from it. NWDC members held in common a respect for material and process, whether they worked in metal, clay, wood, or textiles. They also shared a common problem—finding opportunities to show and sell what they made. There were few craft stores, and galleries that exhibited craftworks were unknown. The series of wholesale and retail fairs that today provide national marketing opportunities for craftspeople were yet to come, although the summer craft fair in Bellevue was already established. Gift shops and modern furniture stores offered the only other sales opportunities.

Was there a distinctive Northwest style, even at the beginning? Because Seattle trades and enjoys cultural interactions with Asian nations, it is not surprising to find influences from Asia, especially China and Japan. Robert Sperry, founding member of NWDC, was first respected as a potter for his references to Japanese traditional pottery and its surface calligraphic decoration. Because he taught at the University of Washington, and eventually headed the ceramics department, his influence was especially important. And furniture making, in the hands of Evert Sodergren, another NWDC founding member, was clearly locked into the Scandinavian Modern perspective so pervasive in the 1950s. (Sodergren's stylistic migration to Japanese/Korean *tansu* chests came later.) The 1950s were about being "modern" in whatever way one might perceive it.

At the end of NWDC's first decade, the world of art and design began to change as the world itself became a smaller place. Montana potter Peter Voulkos, respected for his masterfully thrown functional forms, was

introduced to Zen attitudes toward clay in 1952 by the Japanese potter Shoji Hamada and the British potter Bernard Leach, who were visiting the United States. He constructed, collapsed, slashed, and combined ceramic forms to create sculptural works that echoed the new style in painting, abstract expressionism. Soon, others working in clay also abandoned the brush-decorated, matte-glazed brown pot to explore more sculptural directions. In the Northwest, both Robert Sperry and Ken Shores (in Portland) experimented with abstract expressionism in their sculptural forms.

Margaret DePatta, the California jeweler, usually receives credit for "freeing the stone from bondage" by treating polished river pebbles—not just faceted gemstones—as equals of their metal mounts and allowing them to move with the wearer. The jewelry of Ramona Solberg and Orville Chatt exemplifies similar efforts in the Northwest to use pebbles, colorful leather, and enamel for color and textural interest. And in the eastern United States, weaver Lenore Tawney hung her openwork, woven wall hangings in space, suggesting new sculptural possibilities for textiles. Hella Skowronski and Virginia Harvey introduced new ideas of textile construction in the Northwest. But more change was to come.

Although few Americans even knew where Vietnam was when America went to war there, the hippie movement of the late 1960s introduced Americans to Asian craftwork through block-printed bedspreads from India, the tie-dye methods of Japan and India, and batik from Indonesia. Such patterning processes were seized upon by fiber artists eager for new ideas, and the national Surface Design Movement of the 1970s incorporated this sampling of Asian textile techniques. The richly patterned fabrics found elegant application in artful garments, and the Wearable Art movement was born.

"Jewelry, too, is entering upon a revolutionary phase in which the clean, hard and precise forms of the now-traditional 'modern' style are being abandoned for new conceptions, for shapes and surfaces which are not unlike those being developed in contemporary pottery."

—GERVAIS REED, 1962

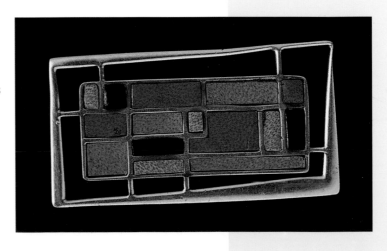

RUSSELL DAY
Pin/Pendant
1955
Silver, forged and fabricated
5 x 4½ in., plus neck cord

HELLA SKOWRONSKI
Untitled Wall Hanging (detail)
1950s
Jute, dyed; leno construction
86 x 16 in., at widest point

Other areas of American crafts were experiencing similar design infusions. While fiber artists incorporated exotic dyeing and patterning processes such as *plangi* and *shibori* into their artistic vocabulary, *mokume gane* and *keumbo* broadened patterning and color possibilities for metalsmiths. Potters, accustomed to using mostly earthenware or stoneware clays, discovered the rich Asian heritage of porcelain and inlays of colored clays. Traditional Japanese glazes were already known, but potters soon began to build wood-fired *anagama* kilns, so large that several potters could combine their wares for a single firing. Raku and other methods such as pit firing opened up new decorative possibilities. The world of crafts was becoming a richer, more varied place as craftspeople backpacked around the globe and studied a burgeoning number of periodicals reporting on the new techniques or attended workshops to learn them.

A radical departure from the functional traditions of clay was seen first in California, where Robert Arneson, teaching at the University of California, Davis, imbued his work with humor, irony, political commentary, and outright vulgarity. He and his students were soon identified as the California Funk Ceramics movement. They were not alone. In Seattle, the University of Washington became almost as well known for the sometimes outrageous ceramic sculpture made by professor Howard Kottler and students Patti Warashina and Fred Bauer.

Craft programs in universities and art schools not only permitted students to examine craft techniques but enabled them to learn sculptural concepts, drawing, printmaking, and painting. That cross-fertilization in the visual arts is especially evident in objects made by NWDC members for this exhibition.

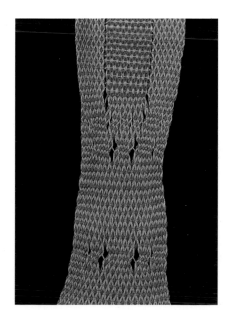

We are a nation without a single governing national style or even pronounced regional ones in our visual arts. We are from everywhere, and we have access to the same resources. Whether their forebears moved here from Singapore or Salzburg, craftspeople in America share their knowledge, and their friendship, with others in the field. So we see interesting juxtapositions of ancient techniques

and contemporary ideas given new currency through a maker's ingenuity. And let us not discount the American fascination with technology.

Today, unlike fifty years ago, furniture makers may inlay colorful resins or veneer imported exotic woods to add elements of luxury to their furniture (while usually remaining mindful of rainforest protection). Refractory metals such as titanium and niobium migrated from the space program into jewelers' studios along with precious-metal and polymer clays. Color photocopy images are regularly transferred to fabric to decorate quilts or enliven panels of glass fused to steel.

During the past half-century, craft has changed and broadened. Hundreds of years after tapestry's heyday in Europe as a rich pictorial medium by which to record myth and history, it survives but with fresh imagery. Handmade paper and felt, esteemed craft traditions elsewhere in the world, were reinvigorated in the 1970s as media for individual expression. Both are represented here. Likewise, the process of forging steel into decorative objects had fallen into decline after the automobile made blacksmiths obsolete. Then, in 1970, Southern Illinois University at Carbondale hosted a workshop at which a blacksmith demonstrated traditional processes to jewelers, which led to a rebirth of

art metalsmithing. And in the 1980s, wood turning moved from the hobbyist's basement into the art museum. Today, there are almost as many avocational turners as there are potters and weavers. Wood turning, like other fields, now has its own national organization as well as an organization of those who collect the work.

REBECCA ROUSH
Corvus Seattlensis #2
Beads, sequins, felt, crows
feet, embroidery, piping
27 x 27 x 1 in.

But where is glass in this fifty-year-old organization? The Puget Sound region boasts the largest concentration of glass artists in the world, surpassing even Venice, the historical center for glass. Perhaps NWDC has few glass artists among its members because the region's glass community is so large, and opportunities to show and sell glass art so ripe, that membership in an all-media craft organization has no appeal for these artists. There are no NWDC members who blow glass, yet the medium is well represented by those who use glass in their work. Some artists compose objects out of tiny glass beads, and other NWDC members fuse glass into functional objects or jewelry.

There is a strong tradition in the Northwest of incorporating cast-off objects or materials or using new objects for other purposes. Ramona Solberg, active throughout the history of the organization as a teacher and maker, became the exemplar of the creative reuse of found objects in jewelry. Her former students, Ron Ho (see p. 43) and Laurie Hall (see p. 39)—who were also admired teachers—are among the NWDC members who continue the tradition. Others add the patterning of colorfully printed used tin or discarded bread wrappers and found paper to their objects. Carolyn Price Dyer spins printed papers in her pictorial weavings, and Robert Purser (see p. 63) continues to compose arresting wall works from both new and used elements.

"[NWDC] members' interest in the group has continued from the beginning, with monthly meetings providing a focal point for communicating with each other and those outside the craft community. And never in the group's history has there been a dormant period. The organization sponsored some of the region's earliest successful art auctions as well as seminars and other educational events. Members appear regularly on television programs, and in the late '50s the group ran a craft shop for a brief period. Generosity has been a hallmark of the group among its members as well as toward the community, where they have supported many projects in the arts with both hard work and funds. Many members have also been active throughout the United States and Europe as board members, as volunteers and delegates to national organizations, in major art exhibitions, and as subjects of articles in recognized publications.

"Exhibitions of members' work have been a principal activity from the beginning, but accelerating in frequency starting around 1975. Probably the most dynamic exhibition occurred when the group was finally included in Century 21 in Seattle in 1962, the culmination of several years of pressure on the Fair's administrative officers who seemed to have heard of the value of painting and sculpture, but who had not yet learned about the wonders of contemporary crafts. After a dynamic and popular six months' run, NWDC was instrumental in transferring the installation into what was to become, and still is today, the Northwest Craft Center at Seattle Center. If one were to compare the work in those earliest exhibitions with that in today's exhibitions, one would see a very great difference in the character of the work presented. There are many new techniques and materials, but the greatest change has been in conceptual approaches, with the shift in direction away from purely functional work to sculptural forms, a trend most noticeable since the early '60s. However, it is becoming obvious that today there is awakening a renewed dynamism and stress on originality among many makers of functional works."

LAMAR HARRINGTON, DIRECTOR EMERITUS, HENRY ART GALLERY, UNIVERSITY OF WASHINGTON, AND DIRECTOR AND CHIEF CURATOR, BELLEVUE ART MUSEUM, NORTHWEST DESIGNER-CRAFTSMEN: THE FIRST THIRTY YEARS, 1985

It is clear then, that craft is no longer defined by the production of functional objects or by the use of materials such as fiber, wood, metal, clay, and glass. Though sculpture, assemblage, and collage are recognized areas within the fine arts, combinations of materials sometimes confound categorization in the crafts. "Mixed media" is, consequently, something of a catch-all term.

Dexterity in shaping diverse materials into art objects helps to blur the boundaries between craft and art. Craft has never been exclusively about function but about the expression of an individual working alone or within the traditions of a community. Most craftspeople are initially attracted to a single discipline, and however many other processes they may master, the materiality of their objects helps to define them as craftmakers.

Freedom to cross the boundaries of material or process exemplifies craft today. Consider the diverse containers and sculptures so loosely categorized as baskets because of their structure. Polly Adams Sutton

uses the material most traditional to basketry in the Northwest, cedar strips, but her creations hardly resemble Indian baskets. Jan Hopkins uses plant materials, too—sometimes such oddities as grapefruit peel—while the material for Fran Reed's containers is fish skin from Alaska (see p. 64). Marilyn Moore chooses wire, Jill Nordfors Clark (see p. 59) works with gut, and Dona Anderson is comfortable with a variety of materials.

Despite the incursions of modern technology, craft traditions have not been lost in fifty years but have instead been enlarged and reinvigorated. The objects selected for this exhibition clearly demonstrate that the handmade is no longer exclusively utilitarian. In fact, the majority of objects here invite contemplation for their artistry alone. It's no crime to be merely beautiful, but increasingly, objects made from the materials and with the processes associated with craft are also about something.

MARILYN MOORE
Full Bloom
2002
Twined wire basket
5½ x 12 x 11 in.

"*The root of the problem for art/craft parity still exists in the art history departments of our nation's colleges and universities. The history and criticism of the crafts is little developed and understood and only rarely offered. Few faculty are prepared to teach these subjects, and if no students are taught, there will continue to be no faculty—it is a circular problem. As a result, most museum curators and critics are not knowledgeable, and therefore, cannot be inspirational in choosing or reviewing exhibitions, or in educating museum boards and collectors. But the winds have obviously changed. It is only a matter of continued advocacy and time.*"

—LAMAR HARRINGTON,
1985

POLLY ADAMS SUTTON
Hoop
2002
Cedarbark, wire basket
15 x 7½ x 5½ in.

JAN HOPKINS
Triads
2000
Alaskan yellow cedar bark,
agave leaves, waxed linen
10 x 11½ x 11 in.

DONA ANDERSON
Lipstick
2003
Fiber
23 x 10 x 4½ in.

It has been significant to the integration of craft with fine art that content has become more apparent, and important. It seems somewhat ironic that abstract expressionism in painting, which denied the representation of human form and the stories we might associate with it, grew into the most recognizable modern art movement in the 1950s. Craft took another decade or so to move in the other direction—representing ideas while perhaps denying beauty.

This survey of current work by NWDC members reflects the larger national field. Whether functional or not, there is quality work that exemplifies the continuity of craft tradition wedded to contemporary expression. Craft membership organizations established after NWDC began to use "artist craftsmen" in their names, recognizing that artistry is not constrained by function, material, and process. It seems somewhat odd, then, that new museums are adding the word "design" to their names (Mint Museum of Craft + Design, San Francisco Museum of Craft and Design) and some existing institutions have decided to drop "craft" altogether, such as the American Craft Museum in New York, which has been renamed the Museum of Arts and Design. For NWDC, the word "designer" has come around again after fifty years! As we look forward to the next fifty years, the one thing certain is change.

LLOYD E. HERMAN

Guest curator, Looking Forward Glancing Back
Founding director (1971-86), Renwick Gallery, Smithsonian American Art Museum,
Smithsonian Institution

"Art is an expression of beauty in every manmade thing--whether it be a sculpture, an automobile, a house or a bridge, an industrial building or a photograph, a table-setting or a chair, exquisite jewelry or a drinking fountain."

—NWDC FOUNDING MEMBER
RUSSELL DAY, "ART IN
CONTEMPORARY LIVING,"
WASHINGTON EDUCATION, 1962

RON ADAMS
Rainbow Road Rattle
2002
Mixed media and found
objects
17 x 4 x 4 in.

POLLY ADAMS SUTTON
Hoop
2002
Cedarbark, wire basket
15 x 7½ x 5½ in.

RUTH ALLAN
Earth Orb
2003
Porcelain
10½ x 16½ in.

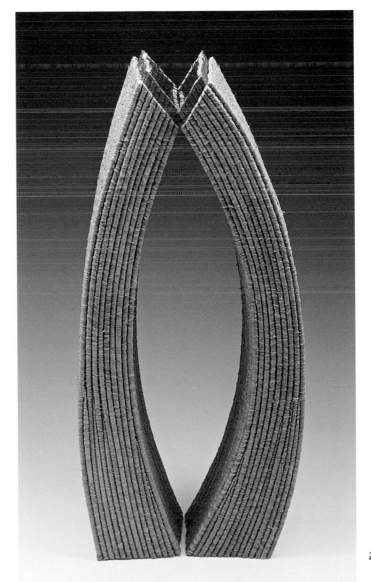

DONA ANDERSON
Lipstick
2003
Fiber
23 x 10 x 4½ in.

PHILLIP BALDWIN
Salad Serving Set
2001
Sterling, sterling/copper
mokume
10¼ x 3⅜ x ¾ in. each

JUDY BARNES BAKER
Tempted and Tried
2003
Paper, ink, paint, leaves,
silicone, glass, grout
28 x 25 in.

DINA BARZEL
Heavy Load
2000
Mixed media, fabric, clay
20 x 20 x 18 in.

LANNY BERGNER
Blue Niki
2003
Gourds, glass frit, wire,
silicone, screen
35 x 17 x 16 in.

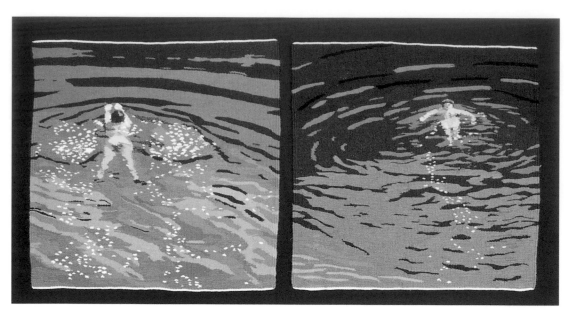

CEILIA BLOMBERG
Swimming in the Shadows
2003
Tapestry
Two panels, 19½ x 19½ in.
each

DANIELLE BODINE
Cocoons-Construction Series
2003
Mixed media
Six cocoons, 12 x 5 in. each

FLORA BOOK
Jaynes Ribbon
2002
Sterling silver and glass
50 x 1½ in.

ERIKA CARTER
Nest XVI
2002
Quilt
71½ x 42 in.

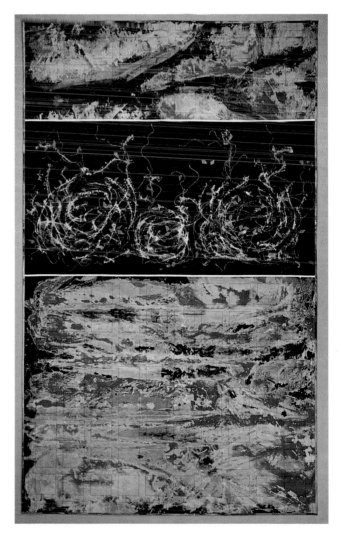

VIRGINIA CAUSEY
Stone Carrier Neckpiece 3
2003
Vintage and Japanese seed
beads
18 x 1½ x ½ in.

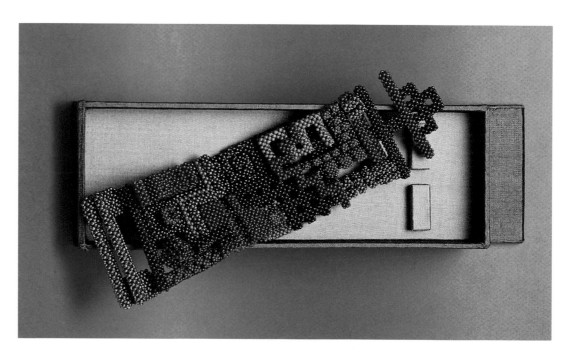

DAVID CHATT
October Bracelet
2003
Beadwork
1½ x 8½ x ½ in.

GINNY CONROW
Yawning Vase
2003
Porcelain
10 x 7 x 2½ in.

GLORIA E. CROUSE
Tossed Salad
2001
Hand-tufted/sculpted
wool on cotton
92 x 80 x 1 in.

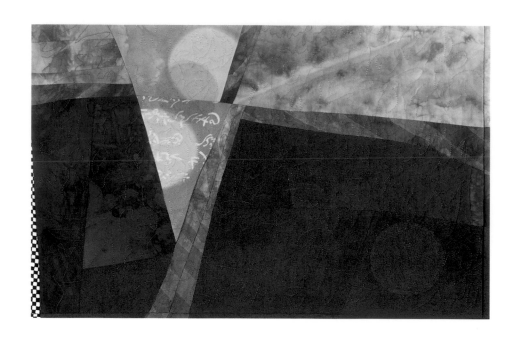

JEANNETTE DENICOLIS
MEYER
Night Words
2003
Quilt
22 x 14½ in.

WENDY ANNE
DEROUX
Smog Alert
2000
Clay, high fire reduction
6 x 8 x 5 in.

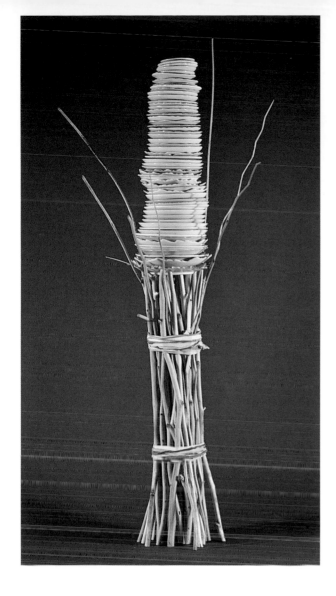

MIKE DEVOE
Earthquake Indicator
2003
Mixed media
39½ x 9 x 7 in.

LYNN DI NINO
Unflappable
2003
Concrete
32 x 16 x 18 in.

CAROLYN PRICE DYER
Theatre of the Birds/Yellow
2003
Tapestry, spun paper
18 x 18 x 1 in.

GRETCHEN ECHOLS
Seasons of the Muse: Focus
2003
Quilted textile, applique
33¼ x 33¼ in.

NANCY N. ERICKSON
Bear Series, #129 Siblings
2002
Oil paintsticks on archival
paper
26 x 40 in.

BENGT ERIKSON
A New Leaf
2003
Tapestry
36 x 37 in.

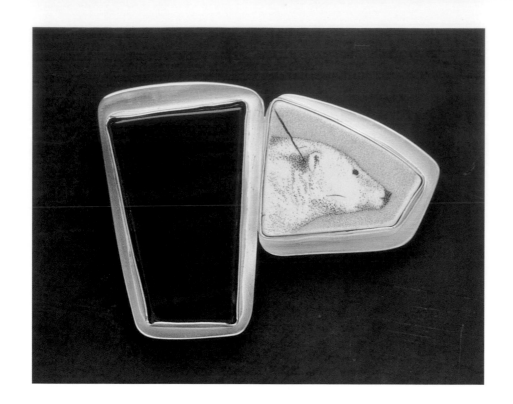

KATHLEEN FAULKNER
Polar Bear
2003
Scrimshaw brooch
1½ x 2 in.

DAVID FRENCH
Interplay
2003
Oil on carved wood
11 x 11 x 9 in.

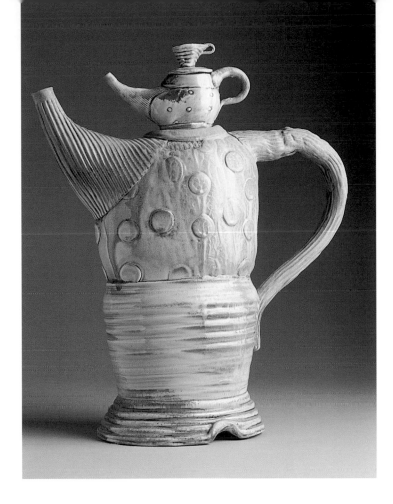

GINA FREUEN
Polka Water Vessel with Teapot Companion
2003
Wood fired porcelain
21½ x 18 x 7 in.

ZIA GIPSON
Cruciform
2002
Handmade felt
60 x 38 in.

NOBLE GOLDEN
Coltrane
2001
Woven paper
39 x 32 in.

BOBBI GOODBOY
Beaded Necklace
2003
Antique Italian beads
8 x 12 in.

NAN GOSS
Landscape No. 36 & 37
2003
Paper on canvas
30 x 70 in.

LAURIE J. HALL
The Rake's Progress
2003
Sterling silver, oak
16 x 6 x 1 in.

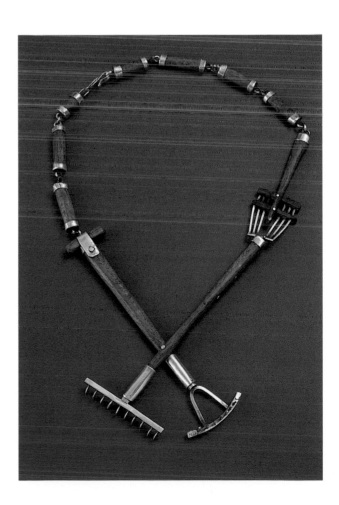

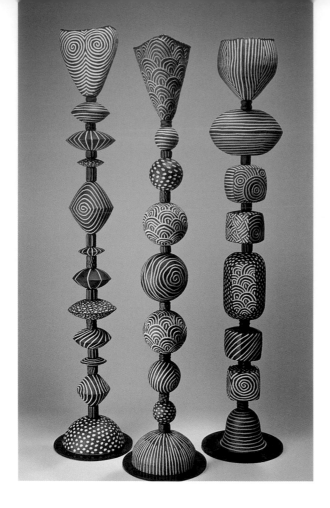

LARRY HALVORSEN
Large Totems
2003
Ceramic
78 x 82 x 18 in.

LIZA HALVORSEN
Many Moons
2003
Ceramic, terracotta
31 x 4 x 3 in. each

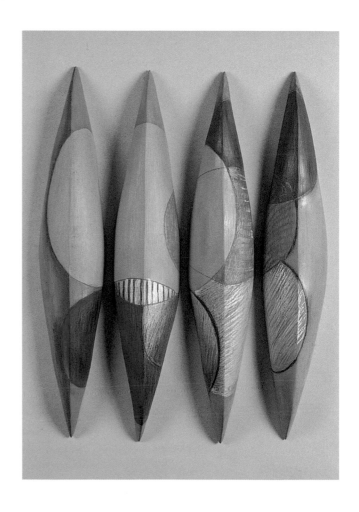

MARIE HASSETT
Body Language
2003
Fiber assemblage
23 x 16 in.

NANCY CLARKE
HEWITT
Astro Rocks
2003
Rubber, silver, horn
8 x 7 x 1 in.

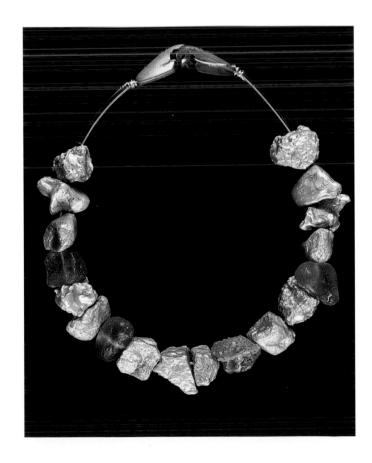

JEAN HICKS
Red Hat Project
2002
Handmade felt
Dimensions variable

PEGGY HITCHCOCK
Rhino and Company
2003
Enamel on copper
14½ x 21 in.

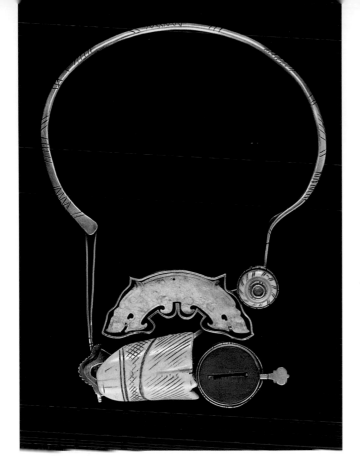

RON HO

Looking Forward, Glancing Back -
NWDC 50th Celebration Necklace
2003
Jade, ivory bead, ivory netsuke,
optometrist implement with forged
and fabricated silver
8½ x 6 x 1½ in.

KATHERINE
HOLZKNECHT

Modern Loutrophoros
2000
Aluminum, brass,
copper wire
46 x 19 x 5 in.

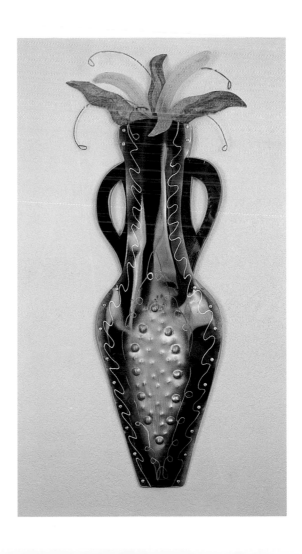

JAN HOPKINS
Triads
2000
Alaskan yellow cedar bark,
agave leaves, waxed linen
10 x 11½ x 11 in.

ROGER H. HORNER
Pair of Salad Servers
2003
Sterling silver
9 x 2¼ in. each

WENDY HUHN

Protection

2001

Mixed media textile

19 x 14 x ½ in.

LARS HUSBY

*Post Apocalyptic Hi-Rise
City Block*

2002

Glazed stoneware and
wood

20 x 30 x 26 in.

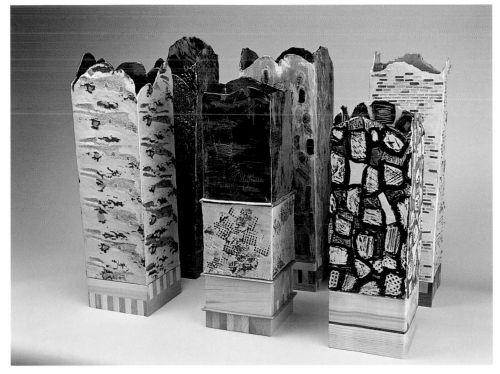

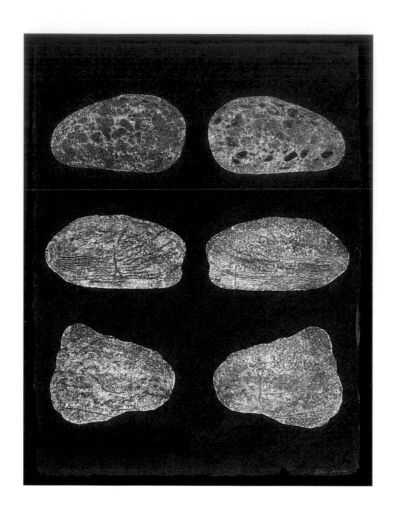

LOIS JAMES
Reversal
2003
Pulp painting on handmade
paper
28 x 22 in.

ANN JOHNSTON
New Growth
2002
Fiber
40 x 33 in.

KAREN KAUFMAN
Interdit
2003
Woven shibori in cotton
21 x 25 in.

JUNE KERSEG-HINSON

Story Bundles of a Changing Culture
2003
Bamboo, paper, wire
82 x 32 x 18 in.

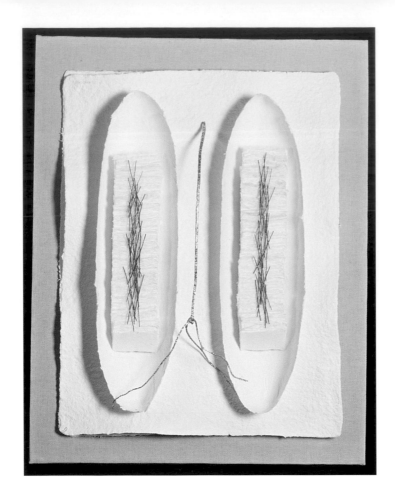

CALVIN KILLGORE
Untitled I
Paper
38½ x 49 x 5 in.

JOHN KILLMASTER
Sisters
2001
Enamel on steel
10 x 8 in.

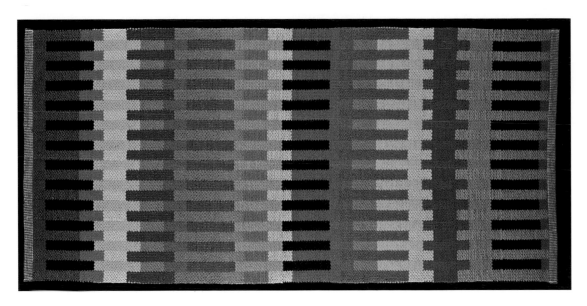

PATTI KING
Full Circle
2003
Double weave wool rug
31 x 65 in.

DIANE KURZYNA
Three Musicians (Klezmorim)
2002
Mixed media, recycled objects
approx. 48 x 36 x 12 in.

BARBARA LEE SMITH
*After the Fall/There Will
Be Spring*
2002
Mixed media
60 x 72 in.

PAUL LEWING
Switchback
2002
Porcelain tile
33 x 21 in.

EUGENE LEWIS
One Step at a Time
2002
Clay, low fire reduction
22⅜ in. diameter

MARTY LOVINS
Untitled
2002
Mixed media construction
11½ x 8½ x 1½ in.

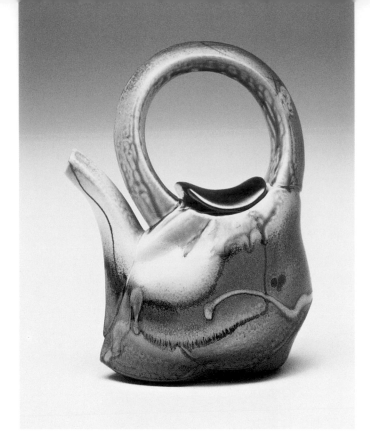

LOREN LUKENS
Altered Teapot
2003
Porcelain
12 x 9 x 4 in.

ANITA LUVERA MAYER
Winter Nights
2002
Fiber
52 x 22 in.

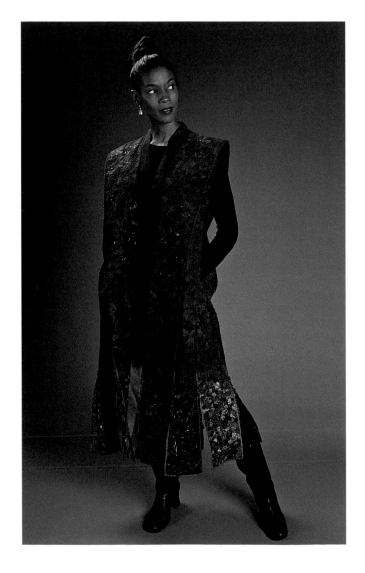

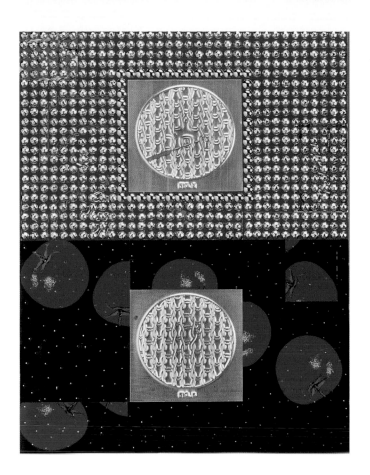

JEAN MANDEBERG
Dropped Stitch
2003
Tin, embossed aluminum,
tacks, wood
22 x 17 x 1 in.

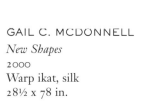

GAIL C. MCDONNELL
New Shapes
2000
Warp ikat, silk
28½ x 78 in.

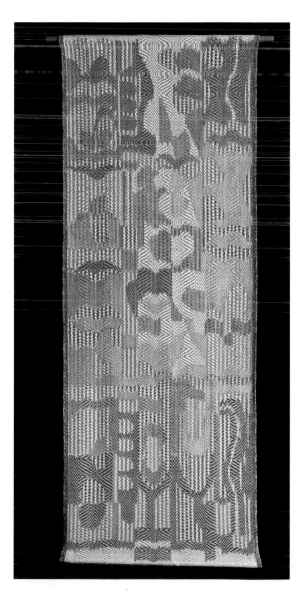

LINDA MCFARLAND
Outcroppings 3,1,2
2000
Block printed and painted
paper on cloth
approx. 55 x 72 in. overall

AGNES MCLIN
Warrior's Mantle
2000
Batik assemblage
40 x 45 x 4 in.

PADDY MCNEELY
*Black Bamboo Stacking
Container*
2003
Porcelain and bamboo
10½ x 10 in.

LARRY METCALF
An Entry
2001
Mixed media
24 x 12 x 12 in.

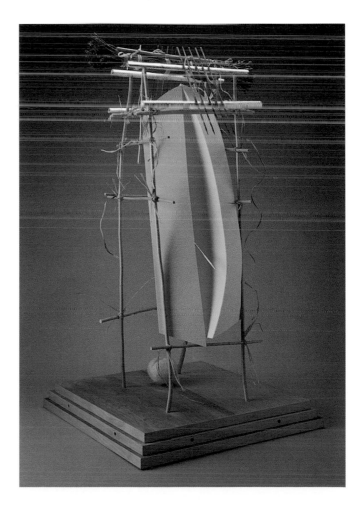

C.A. MICHEL
Untitled
2001
Basketry, black mohair, linen,
feathers
5¼ x 8 in.

MARY MOLYNEAUX
Buddha with Trunk
2003
Acrylic, paper, pencil on
wood with found objects
38 x 17½ x 9¾ in.

MARILYN MOORE
Full Bloom
2002
Twined wire basket
5½ x 12 x 11 in.

JO MORGAN
Down to the Sea Again
2002
Hand-spun wool, linen
67 x 29 in.

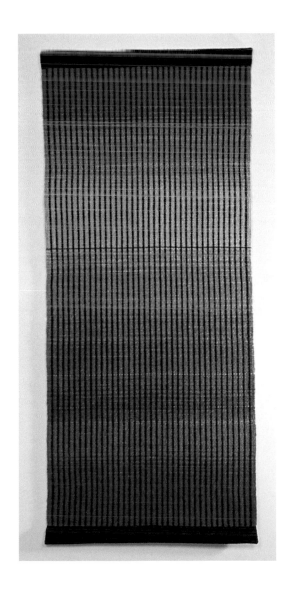

RIKA MOUW
Neck Lace II
2000
Sterling silver, hog gut, silver
leaf
12 x 12 in.

DON MYHRE
Watch It
2003
Mixed media
31 x 28¾ x 11½ in.

ERIC NELSEN
Caravans of Connoisseurs
2003
Clay, anagama fired
29 x 22 x 16 in.

JILL NORDFORS CLARK
Take Flight
2003
Needle lace, hog gut,
weeping willow
26 x 8½ in.

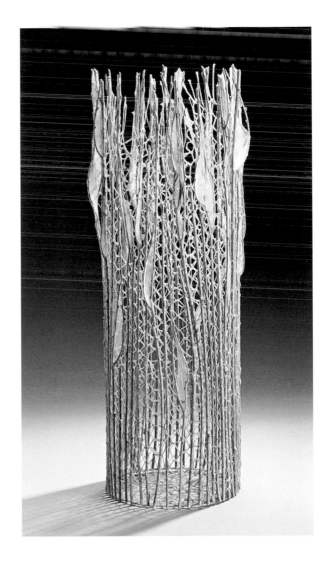

INGE NORGAARD
Life Interrupted #9
2002
Tapestry
22 x 35 in.

PETER OLSEN
Square Dish
2003
Soda-fired stoneware
9 x 9 x 2 in.

JACK OSIER
Textured Teapot
2003
Ceramic
18 x 18 in.

NANCY POBANZ
Stones Hold Secrets
2003
Cigar box, soil pigment from
Steens Mountain, handmade
papers and
hand-felted wool
11¼ x 6¾ x 1¾ in. (closed)

ANNE PRACZUKOWSKI
Rattles - Millenium Markings
2000-2003
Bronze, copper, wood
10 x 3½ in.

MARY PRESTON
Rhythms of Africa: Giraffe
2001
Mixed media, collage
8 x 8 in.

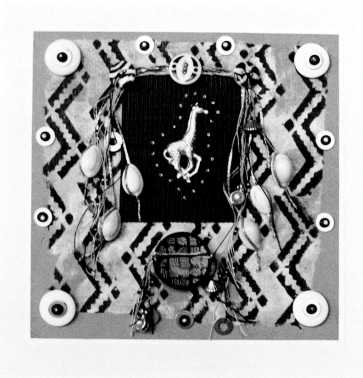

DONNA PRICHARD
Freya's Coat
2001
Textile
50 x 52 in.

ROBERT PURSER
Metallica I (detail)
2003
Sewn paper and wire
26 x 26 x 4 in.

FRAN REED
More or Less
2003
Halibut skin, salmon skin, hog
gut, fern
10 x 14 x 14 in.

DOUGHLAS REMY
Proscenium
2003
Mixed media assemblage
36 x 36 x 2 in.

SUE ROBERTS
Hat Family
2002
Clay, encaustic
23 x 16 x 13 in.

KATHY ROSS
Lost At Sea
2003
Bronze
13 in. diameter

REBECCA ROUSH
Corvus Seattlensis #2
Beads, sequins, felt, crows feet,
embroidery, piping
27 x 27 x 1 in.

R. LEON RUSSELL
Constellation
2003
Sterling silver
9½ x 6 x 6 in.

V. SCHOTTLANDER
Cirque d'Asian
2003
Handwoven grass, felt globes
11 x 14 in.

C.A. SCOTT
Cool
2003
Steel
51 x 20 x 18 in.

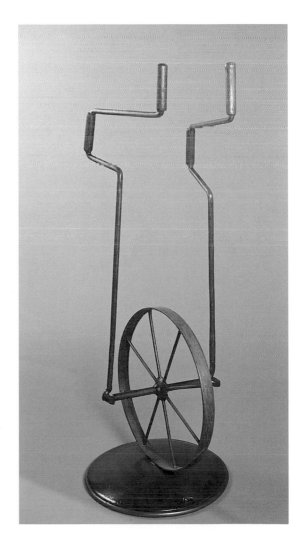

SAM SCOTT
Black and White Jar with Handles
2002
Porcelain
12 in.

SALLY A.
SELLERS

By and Large
2002
Fiber
39½ x 55 x ½ in.

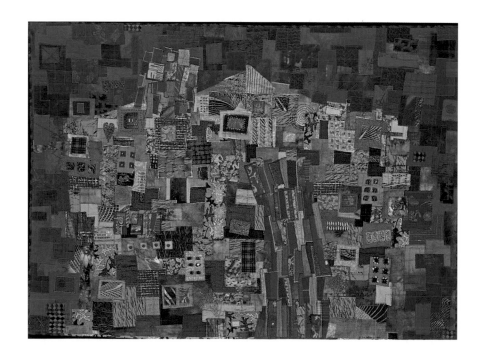

PATTY SGRECCI
Entwined
2003
Carved wood, wire
28 x 17 x 2 in.

BARBARA SKELLY
It Needs More Red
2003
Cloisonne enamel,
wood
6 x 10 x 4 in.

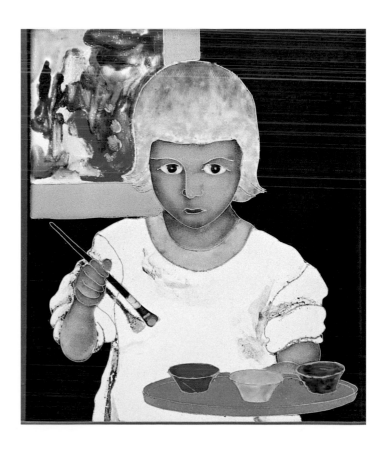

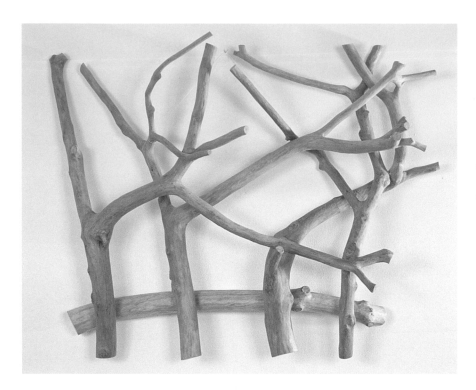

DENISE SNYDER
Silhouette in Apple Wood
2002
Apple and lilac wood
32 x 25 x 13 in.

RAMONA
SOLBERG

X&O Necklace
2003
Silver, pierced shells
10 x 8 x ¼ in.

DIXIE STANTON
Necklace
2003
Silver, trade beads
6 in. wide

BRIAN SWANSON

*Granite Topped
Corner Table*
2002
Granite, steel
33 x 17 x 17 in.

KATHERINE SYLVAN
Arabesque
2003
Fiber
30 x 55 x 3 in.

BONNIE TARSES
Words in Color
2003
Mixed media
28 x 12 in.

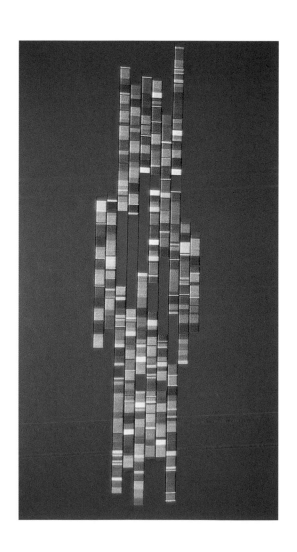

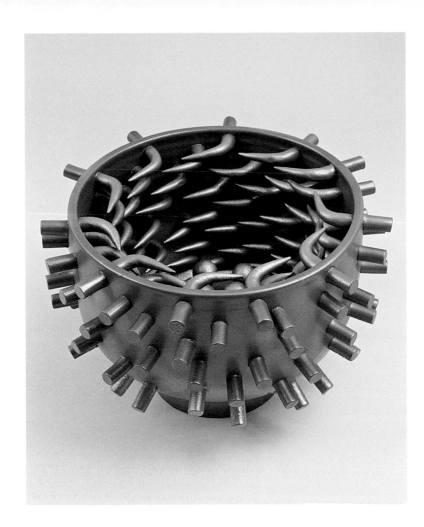

DAVID TRAYLOR
Filled Vessel
2003
Ceramic
12 x 9 x 9 in.

JEAN TUDOR
Vacant City Lot
2002
Enamel on steel
11½ x 11½ in.

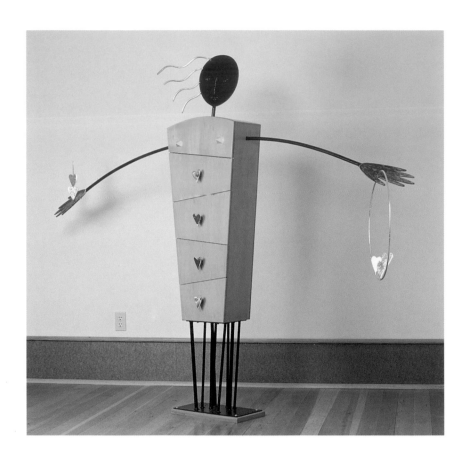

MICHELE VAN SLYKE
Plenty of Love to Store and Play With
2000
Steel, wood
70 x 96 x 12 in.

BARBARA
WALKER

Absorption/Reflection
2003
Silk, rayon
64 x 8 in. each

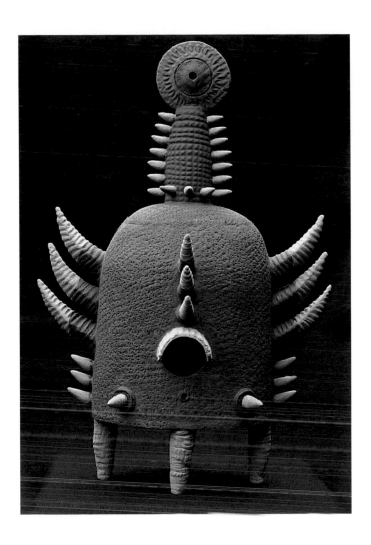

STEWART WONG

Tzaraxia
2003
Stained and glazed terracotta
13½ x 9 x 7½ in.

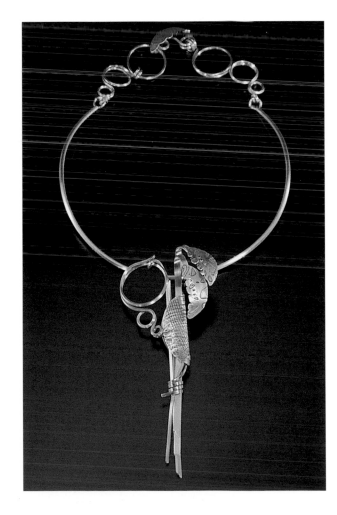

BETH WYATT

Spirit Leaf #7 Necklace
2003
Sterling silver
12½ x 6½ x ½ in.

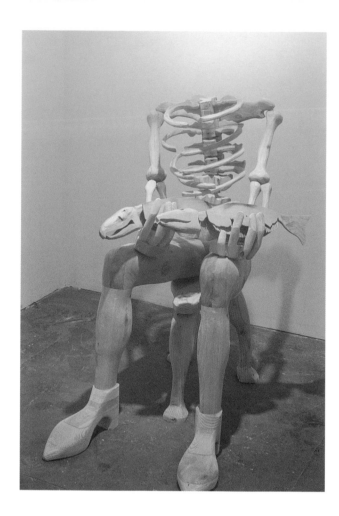

OTTO YOUNGERS
Benzene & Tolvene
2002
Wood
48 x 36 x 36 in.

D. LOWELL
ZERCHER

Off the Grid
2002
Ash, paint, dye
16 x 6 x 6 in.

COMPLETE CHECKLIST OF THE EXHIBITION

All works lent by the artist unless otherwise noted.

RON ADAMS

Rainbow Road Rattle, 2002
Mixed media and found objects
17 x 4 x 4 in.

POLLY ADAMS SUTTON

Hoop, 2002
Cedarbark, wire basket
15 x 7½ x 5½ in.

RUTH ALLAN

Earth Orb, 2003
Porcelain
10½ x 16½ in.

DONA ANDERSON

Lipstick, 2003
Fiber
23 x 10 x 4½ in.

PHILLIP BALDWIN

Roman Table, 2001
Aluminum, glass, brass
48 x 32 x 16 in.

PHILLIP BALDWIN

Salad Serving Set, 2001
Sterling, sterling/copper mokume
10¼ x 3⅜ x ¾ in. each

JUDY BARNES BAKER

Tempted and Tried, 2003
Paper, ink, paint, leaves, silicone, glass, grout
28 x 25 in.

DINA BARZEL

Heavy Load, 2000
Mixed media, fabric, clay
20 x 20 x 18 in.
Courtesy of Francine Seders Gallery

LANNY BERGNER

Blue Niki, 2003
Gourds, glass frit, wire, silicone, screen
35 x 17 x 16 in.

LANNY BERGNER

Orange Branch, 2003
Gourds, glass frit, wire, silicone, screen
20 x 31 x 30 in.

CECILIA BLOMBERG

Swimming in the Shadows, 2003
Tapestry
Two panels, 19½ x 19½ in. each

DANIELLE BODINE

Cocoons-Construction Series, 2003
Mixed media
Six cocoons, 12 x 5 in. each

FLORA BOOK

Jaynes Ribbon, 2002
Sterling silver and glass
50 x 1½ in.
Courtesy of Facère Gallery

FRIKA CARTER

Nest XVI, 2002
Quilt
71½ x 42 in.

VIRGINIA CAUSEY

Stone Carrier Neckpiece 3, 2003
Vintage and Japanese seed beads
18 x 1½ x ½ in.

DAVID CHATT

October Bracelet, 2003
Beadwork
1½ x 8½ x ½ in.

ORVILLE CHATT

Brooch
ca. 1960
Sterling silver
1 x 2 in.

GINNY CONROW

Yawning Vase, 2003
Porcelain
10 x 7 x 2½ in.

GLORIA E. CROUSE

Tossed Salad, 2001
Hand-tufted/sculpted wool on cotton
92 x 80 x 1 in.

RUSSELL DAY

Rug
1950s
Wool, knotted pile
26 x 40 in.
Collection of Russell and Marjorie Day

RUSSELL DAY

Fabric Length
1957
Cotton, screen-printed
36 x 116 in.
Collection of Russell and Marjorie Day

RUSSELL DAY

Pin/Pendant
1955
5 x 4½ in., plus neck cord
Silver, forged and fabricated
Collection of Russell and Marjorie Day

JEANNETTE DENICOLIS MEYER

Night Words, 2003
Quilt
14½ x 22 in.

WENDY ANNE DEROUX

Smog Alert, 2000
Clay, high fire reduction
6 x 8 x 5 in.

MIKE DEVOE

Earthquake Indicator, 2003
Mixed media
39½ x 9 x 7 in.

LYNN DI NINO

Unflappable, 2003
Concrete
32 x 16 x 18 in.

CAROLYN PRICE DYER

Theatre of the Birds/Yellow, 2003
Tapestry, spun paper
18 x 18 x 1 in.

CAROLYN PRICE DYER

Theatre of the Birds/Green, 2003
Tapestry, spun paper
18 x 18 x 1 in.

GRETCHEN ECHOLS

Seasons of the Muse: Focus, 2003
Quilted textile, appliqué
33¼ x 33¼ in.
Collection of Allan Oliver and Gary Simundson

NANCY N. ERICKSON

Bear Series, #129 Siblings, 2002
Oil paintsticks on archival paper
26 x 40 in.

BENGT ERIKSON

A New Leaf, 2003
Tapestry
36 x 37 in.

KATHLEEN FAULKNER

Polar Bear, 2003
Scrimshaw brooch
1½ x 2 in.

BETTY FEVES

Three Figures #4
1955
Stoneware, handbuilt
18 x 12 in.
Collection of Contemporary Crafts Museum and Gallery, Portland, OR

DAVID FRENCH

Interplay, 2003
Oil on carved wood
11 x 11 x 9 in.
Courtesy of Linda Hodges Gallery

GINA FREUEN

Polka Water Vessel with Teapot Companion, 2003
Wood fired porcelain
21½ x 18 x 7 in.

ZIA GIPSON

Cruciform, 2002
Handmade felt
60 x 38 in.

NOBLE GOLDEN

Coltrane, 2001
Woven paper
39 x 32 in.

BOBBI GOODBOY

Beaded Necklace, 2003
Antique Italian beads
8 x 12 in.

NAN GOSS

Landscape No. 36 & 37, 2003
Paper on canvas
30 x 70 in.

LAURIE J. HALL

In My Own Backyard, 2002
Sterling silver, oak, 22k gold bi-metal
16 x 16 x 1 in.
Collection of Clemmer and David Montague

LAURIE J. HALL

The Rake's Progress, 2003
Sterling silver, oak
16 x 6 x 1 in.
Collection of Gale Courtney

LARRY HALVORSEN

Large Totems, 2003
Ceramic
78 x 82 x 18 in.

LIZA HALVORSEN

Many Moons, 2003
Ceramic, terracotta
31 x 4 x 3 in. each

MARIE HASSETT

Body Language, 2003
Fiber assemblage
23 x 16 in.

NANCY CLARKE
HEWITT

Astro Rocks, 2003
Rubber, silver, horn
8 x 7 x 1 in.

JEAN HICKS

Red Hat Project, 2002
Handmade felt

PEGGY
HITCHCOCK

Rhino and Company,
2003
Enamel on copper
14½ x 21 in.

RON HO

*Looking Forward,
Glancing Back—
NWDC 50th
Celebration Necklace*,
2003
Jade, ivory bead,
ivory netsuke,
optometrist imple-
ment with forged and
fabricated silver
8½ x 6 x 1½ in.

RON HO

School Daze, 2003
Bonefish gambling
counters with forged
and fabricated steel
12 x 7 x ½ in.

KATHERINE
HOLZKNECHT

Modern Loutrophoros,
2000
Aluminum, brass,
copper wire
46 x 19 x 5 in.

JAN HOPKINS

Triads, 2000
Alaskan yellow cedar
bark, agave leaves,
waxed linen
10 x 11½ x 11 in.
Collection of Eric and
Barbara Dobkin

ROGER H.
HORNER

Pair of Salad Servers,
2003
Sterling silver
9 x 2¼ in. each

WENDY HUHN

Protection, 2001
Mixed media textile
19 x 14 x ½ in.

LARS HUSBY

*Post Apocalyptic Hi-
Rise City Block*, 2002
Glazed stoneware
and wood
20 x 30 x 26 in.

LOIS JAMES

Reversal, 2003
Pulp painting on
handmade paper
22 x 28 in.

ANN JOHNSTON

New Growth, 2002
Fiber
40 x 33 in.

KAREN KAUFMAN

Interdit, 2003
Woven shibori in
cotton
21 x 25 in.

JUNE KERSEG-
HINSON

*Story Bundles of a
Changing Culture*,
2003
Bamboo, paper, wire
82 x 32 x 18 in.

CALVIN
KILLGORE

Untitled I
Paper
38½ x 49 x 5 in.

JOHN
KILLMASTER

Sisters, 2001
Enamel on steel
10 x 8 in.

PATTI KING

Full Circle, 2003
Double weave
wool rug
31 x 65 in.

DIANE KURZYNA

*Three Musicians
(Klezmorim)*, 2002
Mixed media,
recycled objects
approx. 48 x 36 x 12
in.

BARBARA LEE
SMITH

*After the Fall/
There Will Be Spring*,
2002
Mixed media
60 x 72 in.

PAUL LEWING

Switchback, 2002
Porcelain tile
21 x 33 in.

EUGENE LEWIS

One Step at a Time,
2002
Clay, low fire
reduction
22⅜ in. diameter
Courtesy of Indian
Street Pottery

MARTY LOVINS

Untitled, 2002
Mixed media
construction
11½ x 8½ x 1½ in.

LOREN LUKENS

Altered Teapot, 2003
Porcelain
12 x 9 x 4 in.

ANITA LUVERA
MAYER

Winter Nights, 2002
Fiber
52 x 22 in.

JEAN
MANDEBERG

Dropped Stitch, 2003
Tin, embossed alu-
minum, tacks, wood
22 x 17 x 1 in.

GAIL C.
MCDONNELL

New Shapes, 2000
Warp ikat, silk
28½ x 78 in.

LINDA
MCFARLAND

Outcroppings 3,1,2,
2000
Block printed and
painted paper on
cloth
approx. 55 x 72 in.
overall

AGNES MCLIN

Warrior's Mantle,
2000
Batik assemblage
40 x 45 x 4 in.

PADDY MCNEELY

*Black Bamboo Stacking
Container*, 2003
Porcelain and
bamboo
10½ x 10 in.

LARRY METCALF

An Entry, 2001
Mixed media
24 x 12 x 12 in.

C.A. MICHEL

Untitled, 2001
Basketry, black
mohair, linen,
feathers
5¼ x 8 in.

MARY
MOLYNEAUX

Buddha with Trunk,
2003
Acrylic, paper, pencil
on wood with found
objects
38 x 17½ x 9¾ in.
Courtesy of Ballard
Fetherston Gallery

MARILYN MOORE

Full Bloom, 2002
Twined wire basket
5½ x 12 x 11 in.

JO MORGAN

*Down to the Sea
Again*, 2002
Hand-spun wool,
linen
67 x 29 in.

RIKA MOUW

Neck Lace II, 2000
Sterling silver, hog
gut, silver leaf
12 x 12 in.

DON MYHRE

Watch It, 2003
Mixed media
31 x 28¾ x 11½ in.

ERIC NELSEN

*Caravans of
Connoisseurs*, 2003
Clay, anagama fired
29 x 22 x 16 in.

JILL NORDFORS
CLARK

Take Flight, 2003
Needle lace, hog gut,
weeping willow
26 x 8½ in.

INGE NORGAARD

Life Interrupted #9,
2002
Tapestry
22 x 35 in.

PETER OLSEN

Square Dish, 2003
Soda-fired stoneware
9 x 9 x 2 in.

JACK OSIER

Textured Teapot, 2003
Ceramic
18 x 18 in.

RUTH
PENINGTON

Two Candlesticks
1963
Silver, uncut topaz
6½ x 4 in.
Collection of Caryl
Roman

NANCY POBANZ

Stones Hold Secrets,
2003
Cigar box, soil
pigment from Steens
Mountain, handmade
papers and hand-
felted wool
11¼ x 6¾ x 1¾ in.
(closed)

ANNE
PRACZUKOWSKI

*Rattles - Millenium
Markings*, 2000-2003
Bronze, copper, wood
10 x 3½ in.

MARY PRESTON

*Rhythms of Africa:
Giraffe*, 2001
Mixed media, collage
8 x 8 in.

DONNA PRICHARD

Freya's Coat, 2001
Textile
50 x 52 in.

ROBERT PURSER

Metallica I, 2003
Sewn paper and wire
26 x 26 x 4 in.

FRAN REED

More or Less, 2003
Halibut skin, salmon
skin, hog gut, fern
10 x 14 x 14 in.
Collection of Chris
Arend

DOUGHLAS REMY

Proscenium, 2003
Mixed media
assemblage
36 x 36 x 2 in.

SUE ROBERTS

Hat Family, 2002
Clay, encaustic
23 x 16 x 13 in.

KATHY ROSS

Lost At Sea, 2003
Bronze
13 in. diameter

REBECCA ROUSH

Corvus Seattlensis #2
Beads, sequins, felt,
crows feet, embroi-
dery, piping
27 x 27 x 1 in.

R. LEON RUSSELL

Constellation, 2003
Sterling silver
9½ x 6 x 6 in.

LISEL SALZER

Susan
1950s
Enamel, Limoges
technique
4½ x 4 in.

LISEL SALZER

Mother and Child
1950s
Enamel, Limoges
technique
5½ x 4¼ in.

LISEL SALZER

Hopi Indian
1950s
Enamel, Limoges
technique
3⅛ x 4 in.

LISEL SALZER

Peter
1950s
Enamel, Limoges
technique
5½ x 4 in.

V. SCHOTTLANDER

Cirque d'Asian, 2003
Handwoven grass,
felt globes
11 x 14 in.

C.A. SCOTT

Cool, 2003
Steel
51 x 20 x 18 in.

SAM SCOTT

*Black and White Jar
with Handles*, 2002
Porcelain
12 in.

SALLY A. SELLERS

By and Large, 2002
Fiber
39½ x 55 x ½ in.

FRANCES SENSKA

Ray Bowl
1954
Stoneware, thrown
and glazed
2⅛ x 10½ in.
Collection of
Contemporary Craft
Museum and Gallery,
Portland, OR

PATTY SGRECCI

Entwined, 2003
Carved wood, wire
28 x 17 x 2 in.

KEN SHORES

Little Red I
1962
Stoneware, handbuilt,
acrylic paint
20 in. high
Courtesy of the artist
and Broderick Gallery,
Portland, OR

BARBARA SKELLY

It Needs More Red,
2003
Cloisonne enamel,
wood
6 x 10 x 4 in.

HELLA SKOWRONSKI

Untitled Wall Hanging
1950s
Jute, dyed; leno
construction
86 x 16 in., at widest
point
Collection of Bif
Brigman

DENISE SNYDER

*Silhouette in Apple
Wood*, 2002
Apple and lilac wood
32 x 25 x 13 in.

EVERT SODERGREN

Untitled Pierced Screen
ca. 1957
Walnut, laminated
31 x 39
Collection of Bif
Brigman

EVERT SODERGREN

Untitled Chair
1998 (design
introduced 1953)
Walnut
27 x 28 x 24 in.

RAMONA SOLBERG

Necklace
1953
Champleve enamel
on steel
6 x 4½ x ⅛ in.

RAMONA SOLBERG

X&O Necklace, 2003
Silver, pierced shells
10 x 8 x ¼ in.

ROBERT SPERRY

Untitled Bottle
1959
Stoneware, thrown
and altered, glazed
24 x 15 x 6 in.
Collection of Bif
Brigman

DIXIE STANTON

Necklace, 2003
Silver, trade beads
6 in. wide

BRIAN SWANSON

*Granite Topped
Corner Table*, 2002
Granite, steel
33 x 17 x 17 in.
Courtesy of the artist
and Gallery 24

KATHFRINE SYLVAN

Arabesque, 2003
Fiber
30 x 55 x 3 in.

BONNIE TARSES

Black on Black, 2004
Woven chenille
28 x 84 in.

BONNIE TARSES

Words in Color, 2003
Mixed media
28 x 12 in.

DONALD TOMPKINS

Bracelet Watch
ca. 1957
Silver, forged and
fabricated; watch
movement
3 x 2¼ x 2¼ in.
Collection of Russell
and Marjorie Day

DAVID TRAYLOR

Filled Vessel, 2003
Ceramic
12 x 9 x 9 in.

JEAN TUDOR

Vacant City Lot, 2002
Enamel on steel
11½ x 11½ in.

MICHELE VAN SLYKE

*Plenty of Love to Store
and Play With*, 2000
Steel, wood
70 x 96 x 12 in.

BARBARA WALKER

Absorption/Reflection,
2003
Silk, rayon
64 x 8 in. each

STEWART WONG

Tzaraxia, 2003
Stained and glazed
terracotta
13½ x 9 x 7½ in.

BETH WYATT

*Spirit Leaf #7
Necklace*,
2003
Sterling silver
12½ x 6½ x ½ in.

OTTO YOUNGERS

Benzene & Tolvene,
2002
Wood
48 x 36 x 36 in.

D. LOWELL ZERCHER

Off the Grid, 2002
Ash, paint, dye
16 x 6 x 6 in.

Looking Forward, Glancing Back: Northwest Designer Craftsmen at 50 is sponsored in part by Peoples Bank.

Whatcom Museum program support provided by the City of Bellingham, the Washington State Arts Commission, and the National Endowment for the Arts.

Many thanks to our generous contributors.

WHATCOM MUSEUM OF HISTORY & ART